A Note From Rick Renner

I 0200372

I am on a personal quest to see a "revival of the Bible" so people can establish their lives on a firm foundation that will stand strong and endure the test when the end-time storm winds begin to intensify.

In order to experience a revival of the Bible in your personal life, it is important to take time each day to read, receive, and apply its truths to your life. James tells us that if we will continue in the perfect law of liberty — refusing to be forgetful hearers but determined to be doers — we will be blessed in our ways. As you watch or listen to the programs in this series and work through this corresponding study guide, I trust that you will search the Scriptures and allow the Holy Spirit to help you hear something new from God's Word that applies specifically to your life. I encourage you to be a doer of the Word that He reveals to you. Whatever the cost, I assure you — it will be worth it.

Thy words were found, and I did eat them;
and thy word was unto me the joy and rejoicing of mine heart:
for I am called by thy name, O Lord God of hosts.
— Jeremiah 15:16

Your brother and friend in Jesus Christ,

Rick Renner

Upper Room Realities

Copyright © 2020 by Rick Renner
8316 E. 73rd St.
Tulsa, Oklahoma 74133

Published by Rick Renner Ministries
www.renner.org

ISBN 13: 978-1-68031-684-1

eBook ISBN 13: 978-1-68031-685-8

The emphasis of this lesson:

The Upper Room in the city of Jerusalem serves as an example of what will happen when you surrender your home to the lordship of Jesus Christ. Not only will history be made, but you and your family will make history.

Did you know that there is a room in the city of Jerusalem that is so important it has been included in more than 260 verses of the New Testament? The catalog of significant events that occurred in this place is simply staggering. Since the Fourth Century, this room has been recognized as the historic location where Jesus met regularly with His disciples and where the disciples met regularly with the Holy Spirit and each other for many years after the Church was launched. This place is called the *Upper Room*. It's also called the "Cenacle," which is the Latin word meaning *upper room* and you can still visit it today in Jerusalem.

The Upper Room Is Where...

Jesus served the disciples Communion (John 13).

On the final night Christ was with His disciples, He ate the Passover meal — also known as the Last Supper — and then served them what we now know as Communion. The details of these events that took place in the Upper Room are recorded primarily in the synoptic gospels (Matthew, Mark, and Luke), but John also mentioned this major event in his thirteenth chapter.

Jesus washed the feet of the disciples (John 13:1-17).

After the Passover meal was ended, the Bible says that Christ laid aside His garments, girded Himself with a servant's towel, and washed His disciples' feet — even the feet of Judas Iscariot, the one who betrayed Him. This event took place in the Upper Room.

Jesus taught about the Holy Spirit (John 14-16).

After washing the disciples' feet and predicting His betrayal, Jesus said He would be returning to the Father but that He would be sending the Holy Spirit in His place to live inside each believer. He then described the ministry of the Spirit, including His ability to lead us and guide us into all truth and reveal things yet to come. Christ's teaching on the Holy Spirit took place in the Upper Room.

Jesus prayed His high priestly prayer (John 17).

Just before Christ and His disciples made their way into the Garden of Gethsemane, He took time to pray a priestly prayer on His disciples that were with Him and all those who would believe in Him through their witness. Again and again, He asked the Father to unite us as one, just as He and the Father are one. This priestly prayer was prayed in the Upper Room.

Jesus appeared to the disciples after His resurrection (John 20:19-31).

After Christ was crucified and placed in the tomb of Joseph of Arimathea, the disciples shut themselves in behind locked doors for fear of the Jews. And while they were in hiding, Jesus suddenly came and stood in their midst and revealed Himself to them. He breathed on them and said, "... receive ye the Holy Ghost" (John 20:22). Not once, but twice He appeared to them behind closed doors, and this took place in the Upper Room.

Jesus' disciples gathered after the ascension (Acts 1:9-13).

As the disciples stood on the Mount of Olives, they watched Jesus ascend out of their sight into Heaven. Instantly, two angels appeared and comforted them with the news that Christ would one day return again in like manner. The faithful followers of Jesus then returned to the city of Jerusalem and made their way back to the Upper Room where they continued to pray and seek God.

Jesus sent the 120 to wait for the promise of the Father (Acts 1:4,5).

As a part of His final words to His disciples, Jesus "...commanded them that they should not depart from Jerusalem, but wait for the promise of the Father, which, saith he, ye have heard of me. For John truly baptized with water; but ye shall be baptized with the Holy Ghost not many days hence" (Acts 1:4,5). This commandment was so important it is also recorded in Luke 24:49. Can you guess where the disciples gathered together in Jerusalem? Yes, it was in the Upper Room.

Matthias was chosen to be an apostle (Acts 1:15-26).

As the disciples and followers of Christ faithfully waited in Jerusalem for the promise of the Holy Spirit, the disciples discussed the need to fill the place vacated by Judas the betrayer. Two individuals who had been with Jesus since the day of His baptism were considered, and after a time of prayer, Matthias was selected to fill the position and be counted with the eleven other apostles.

The Holy Spirit descended on the Day of Pentecost (Acts 2:1-4).
Fifty days after Jesus had risen from the grave, the promised gift of the Holy Spirit was poured out on the 120 faithful followers who were obediently waiting in the city of Jerusalem. Instantly, they were all filled with the same Spirit that raised Christ from the dead, and they began to powerfully proclaim in the native tongues of the earth the wonderful works of God. The world would never be the same again, and this took place in the same Upper Room.

The house was physically shaken by the power of God (Act 4:23-31).
Evidently, the Upper Room became one of the first places where the Church congregated after the Day of Pentecost. For instance, after Peter and John were arrested and interrogated by the Jewish leaders and then released, they joined the rest of the believers who were already assembled for a time of prayer in the Upper Room. The Bible says, "And when they had prayed, the place was shaken where they were assembled together..." (Acts 4:31).

Peter went when he was released from prison (Acts 12:12-17).
After Herod had had Peter arrested and imprisoned, the Church prayed without ceasing for him (*see* Acts 12:5). God heard and answered their prayers by sending His angel to set Peter free. After being led out of prison, Peter fully came to his senses and immediately made his way to the Upper Room in Jerusalem where he knew the saints would be gathered in prayer.

The House of Mary, the Mother of John Mark

All the aforementioned events happened in the same place — the Upper Room in Jerusalem. What you may not realize is that the Upper Room was not a public building. It was actually someone's private home! The Bible tells us about a woman named Mary who appears to have been very wealthy and owned a very large and prestigious house in the center of the ancient city of Jerusalem near the temple. The Upper Room was located in her home on the second or third floor.

Scripture also says that this same Mary was the mother of John Mark. Acts 12:12 reveals that when Peter was miraculously delivered from prison by the angel of the Lord, "…he came to the house of Mary the mother of John, whose surname was Mark; where many were gathered together praying."

Think about it. John Mark grew up in his mother Mary's home, and it had been totally dedicated to the Lord. This home was the meeting place for Jesus and His disciples whenever they were in Jerusalem. Thus, John Mark met and got to know all the apostles from his teenage years. More importantly, he grew up knowing Jesus and being in His presence regularly.

If you are a parent, never be afraid of involving your children in ministry. John Mark was exposed to the presence of Jesus and saw firsthand what anointed ministry looked like. Thus, the call of God was birthed in his heart, and he was trained and prepared for ministry at a very early age.

Barnabas Was Mary's Brother, John Mark's Uncle

This same Mary, who was the mother of John Mark, was also the sister of another well-known follower of Christ. His name was *Barnabas*. Paul mentioned this connection in Colossians 4:10, saying, "Aristarchus my fellowprisoner saluteth you, and Marcus, sister's son to Barnabas…." In Greek, the phrase "sister's son" is *anepsios*, which means *nephew* or *cousin*. Thus, Barnabas was the uncle of John Mark.

This helps us understand why Barnabas took the stance he did during his travels with the apostle Paul. The Bible says, "And Barnabas determined to take with them John, whose surname was Mark. But Paul thought not good to take him with them, who departed from them from Pamphylia, and went not with them to the work. And the contention was so sharp between them, that they departed asunder one from the other: and so Barnabas took Mark, and sailed unto Cyprus; and Paul chose Silas, and departed, being recommended by the brethren unto the grace of God" (Acts 15:37-40).

Apparently, John Mark went AWOL and ran home to his mother during one of Paul and Barnabas' missionary stops. Not wanting to be deserted again, Paul opted not to take John Mark on his second missionary journey. Uncle Barnabas, however, wanted to give his young nephew another chance. The disagreement over taking John Mark was so great, Paul and Barnabas parted ways.

Over time John Mark matured, and Scripture informs us that after several years he became Peter's personal assistant. At the end of Peter's first epistle, he wrote, "The church that is at Babylon, elected together with you, saluteth you; and so doth *Marcus my son*" (1 Peter 5:13). John Mark had become a spiritual son to Peter. In fact, he became so valuable to the cause of Christ that Peter dictated his perspective of the Gospel to John Mark. We have come to know this as the gospel of Mark, but it is actually Peter's gospel.

Again, there are more than 260 verses in the New Testament that describe the events that occurred in the Upper Room. This room was located in Mary's house — mother of John Mark and sister of Barnabas. And just like Mary, if you open the doors of your home and dedicate it to Jesus, He will invade your home with His presence and power. He will manifest His miracles and fully display the gifts of His Holy Spirit.

STUDY QUESTIONS

Study to shew thyself approved unto God, a workman that needeth not to be ashamed, rightly dividing the word of truth.
— 2 Timothy 2:15

1. What new insights have you learned in this lesson about the Upper Room in Jerusalem? Name the events that you were unaware of that took place in the Upper Room.
2. What did you discover about Mary — the wealthy widow woman who owned the Upper Room?
3. Mary loved Jesus and willingly opened the doors of her home to Him and His disciples. What has God promised will happen when you welcome Jesus into your home and life? (Consider Revelation 3:20; James 4:8; Psalm 16:8; 145:18; Matthew 11:28-30.)

PRACTICAL APPLICATION

But be ye doers of the word, and not hearers only, deceiving your own selves.
— James 1:22

1. Imagine you are Mary, and Jesus and His disciples are coming to *your* home and regularly spending time with you and your family. What

do you think makes Jesus feel so welcomed and comfortable in your home? How is your family impacted by the presence of Jesus and His disciples?

2. Would Jesus feel welcomed and comfortable coming and staying at your house? Is there anything present or taking place in your home that you feel would repel Him from entering and taking up residence? If so, what is it? What steps can you take to eliminate this obstruction to the presence of God in your home? Take time now to invite Jesus to begin working in your house.

TOPIC

Jesus Wants Your Living Room

SCRIPTURES

1. **Acts 1:4,5** — And, being assembled together with them, commanded them that they should not depart from Jerusalem, but wait for the promise of the Father, which, saith he, ye have heard of me. For John truly baptized with water; but ye shall be baptized with the Holy Ghost not many days hence.

2. **Acts 1:12-17** — Then returned they unto Jerusalem from the mount called Olivet, which is from Jerusalem a sabbath day's journey. And when they were come in, they went up into an upper room, where abode both Peter, and James, and John, and Andrew, Philip, and Thomas, Bartholomew, and Matthew, James the son of Alphaeus, and Simon Zelotes, and Judas the brother of James. These all continued with one accord in prayer and supplication, with the women, and Mary the mother of Jesus, and with his brethren. And in those days Peter stood up in the midst of the disciples, and said, (the number of names together were about an hundred and twenty,) men and brethren, this scripture must needs have been fulfilled, which the Holy Ghost by the mouth of David spake before concerning Judas, which was guide to them that took Jesus. For he was numbered with us, and had obtained part of this ministry.

3. **Acts 20:7,8** — And upon the first day of the week, when the disciples came together to break bread, Paul preached unto them, ready to depart on the morrow; and continued his speech until midnight. And there were many lights in the upper chamber, where they were gathered together.

4. **Acts 1:21-24,26** — Wherefore of these men which have companied with us all the time that the Lord Jesus went in and out among us, beginning from the baptism of John, unto that same day that he was taken up from us, must one be ordained to be a witness with us of his resurrection. And they appointed two, Joseph called Barsabas, who was surnamed Justus, and Matthias. And they prayed, and said, Thou, Lord, which knowest the hearts of all men, shew whether of these two thou hast chosen. ...And they gave forth their lots; and the lot fell upon Matthias; and he was numbered with the eleven apostles.

GREEK WORDS

1. "upper room" — ὑπερῷον (*huperoon*): the highest part of the house; the upper rooms or upper story of a house; a room in the upper part of a house; upper chamber; usually the largest open space in an ancient home

2. "abode" — καταμένω (*katameno*): to settle down and stay; to remain consistently

3. "all" — πάντες (*pantes*): all of them; an all-encompassing word; no one was excluded

4. "continued" — προσκαρτερέω (*proskartereo*): to persevere consistently; pictures intense focus and hard work; constant diligence and effort that never lets up; pictures one who is fixed in a forward position

5. "one accord" — ὁμοθυμαδόν (*homothumadon*): a compound of ὁμοῦ (*homou*) and θυμός (*thumos*); the word ὁμοῦ (*homou*) points to a moment when something happens at one time or simultaneously; the word θυμός (*thumos*) pictures passion; compounded, pictures those who are stirred up, excited, and are at one moment caught up in an eruption of passion; a thrilling moment

6. "prayer" — προσευχή (*proseuche*): close, up-front, intimate contact; coming close to express a wish, desire, prayer, or vow; originally used to depict a person who vowed to give something of great value to God in exchange for a favorable answer to prayer; portrays an individual

who desires to see his prayer answered so desperately that he is willing to surrender everything he owns in exchange for answered prayer; hence, contained in this word is the concept of surrender

7. "with the women" — σὺν γυναιξὶν (*sun gunaixin*): together with women; in partnership with women

8. "and Mary the mother of Jesus" — καὶ Μαριὰμ τῇ μητρὶ τοῦ Ἰησοῦ (*kai Mariam te metri tou Iesou*): literally, "and Mary the mother of Jesus"

9. "and with his brethren" — καὶ σὺν τοῖς ἀδελφοῖς αὐτοῦ (*kai sun tois adelphois autou*): and together with his multiple natural brothers; the word σύν (*sun*) implies partnership with his brothers

10. "guide" — ὁδηγός (*hodegos*): a guide who shows a traveler the safest course through an unknown country; a guide who knows all the paths, tracks, and roads; a guide

11. "numbered" — καταριθμέω (*katarithmeo*): counted; numbered among

12. "with us" — ἐν ἡμῖν (*en hemin*): literally, in us; among us

13. "obtained" — λαγχάνω (*lagchano*): to receive by divine allotment

14. "ministry" — διακονία (*diakonia*): the ministry; from διάκονος (*diakonos*), a high-level servant; in history, sophisticated and highly trained servants who served the needs of others; a servant whose primary responsibility was to serve food and wait on tables; a waiter or waitress who painstakingly attended to the needs, wishes, and desires of his or her client; servants who professionally pleased clients; a type of serving that was honorable, pleasurable, and done in a fashion that made people being served feel as if they were nobility; used to depict those in the ministry

15. "witness" — μάρτυς (*martus*): one summoned to testify in a court of law; pictures the evidence presented in a legal case; a legal witness that was only allowed to speak what he personally knew to be true; could be connected to the idea of suffering because one called to be a witness was required to be faithful to the truth, regardless of any possible acts of retribution that might be carried out against him by those who opposed his witness or wished to suppress the truth; when summoned to be a witness, it was inherently understood that this act could place an individual or his loved ones in jeopardy; thus to be a witness required the highest level of integrity and commitment, as well as a willingness to sacrifice oneself or one's status to uphold the truth

16. "knowest the hearts"— **καρδιογνώστης** (*kardiognostes*): compound of **καρδία** (*kardia*) and **γνώστης** (*gnostes*); the word **καρδία** (*kardia*) depicts the heart or the innermost part of a person; the word **γνώστης** (*gnostes*) means to know like an expert; hence, the heart-knower or the expert of all human hearts

17. "Thou, Lord"— **Σὺ Κύριε** (*Su Kurie*): the word **Σὺ** (*su*) implies intimacy and direct speech; the word **Κύριε** (*Kurie*) is the direct form of **κύριος** (*kurios*), meaning lord or supreme master; in these words are both intimacy and respect

18. "gave forth their lots"— **ἔδωκαν αὐτοῖς, κλήρους** (*edokan autois klerous*): here is pictured a game of dice

SYNOPSIS

As we learned in our first lesson, the Upper Room in Jerusalem was a place where many noteworthy events in the Early Church took place. It is the traditional site where Jesus regularly rendezvoused with His disciples when they were in Jerusalem, and it was recognized as early as the First Century as the place of Pentecost. During the reign of Emperor Hadrian (117 to 138 AD), believers were still meeting in this sacred room, and by the Fourth Century, it had been converted into a church. If you journey to Jerusalem today, you will find it has been nearly perfectly preserved since the Fourteenth Century.

Again, the Upper Room was not a public facility. It was a part of someone's private home, and that someone was named Mary. She was the mother of John Mark, who became Peter's secretary and wrote the gospel of Mark. She was also the sister of Barnabas, Paul's friend and partner in ministry throughout his first missionary journey. It seems Mary was a widow who was financially well-off. Out of her passionate love for Jesus, she threw open the doors of her home to Him and His disciples; and as a result supernatural history was made — and it's still being made in her home today!

The emphasis of this lesson:

If you want to experience upper-room realities in your own space, surrender your place to Jesus. He will invade and occupy your home, bringing His presence, His power, and His glory with Him. He's just waiting for you to invite Him in.

The Disciples 'Abode in the Upper Room'

In Acts 1:4 and 5, we find Jesus giving His disciples some last-minute instructions before returning to Heaven. The Bible says, "And, being assembled together with them, commanded them that they should not depart from Jerusalem, but wait for the promise of the Father, which, saith he, ye have heard of me. For John truly baptized with water; but ye shall be baptized with the Holy Ghost not many days hence."

Not wanting His closest followers to miss out on receiving the priceless, empowering Gift of His Spirit, Jesus commanded them to stay put in Jerusalem. Where did the disciples go when Jesus was done speaking? Scripture says, "Then returned they unto Jerusalem from the mount called Olivet, which is from Jerusalem a sabbath day's journey. And when they were come in, they went up into an upper room, where abode both Peter, and James, and John, and Andrew, Philip, and Thomas, Bartholomew, and Matthew, James the son of Alphaeus, and Simon Zelotes, and Judas the brother of James" (Acts 1:12,13).

Notice Acts 1:13 says that the disciples "abode" in the Upper Room. The word "abode" is the Greek word *katameno*, which means *to settle down and stay; to remain consistently*. The Bible says they *settled down* in the "upper room," which is a translation of the Greek word *huperoon*, and it describes *the highest part of the house; the upper rooms or upper story of a house; a room in the upper part of a house; an upper chamber*. Upper rooms were *usually the largest open spaces in an ancient home*, able to accommodate many people. Such was the case with the Upper Room in Mary's house.

Another example of the word *huperoon* is found in Acts 20:7 and 8 which says, "And upon the first day of the week, when the disciples came together to break bread, Paul preached unto them, ready to depart on the morrow; and continued his speech until midnight. And there were many lights in the upper chamber, where they were gathered together." The phrase "upper chamber" is the same Greek word *huperoon*, which describes *the highest part of a house; the upper rooms or upper story of a house that is the largest open space*.

The Disciples Persevered in Prayer

Returning to Acts 1, the Bible says, "These all continued with one accord in prayer and supplication, with the women, and Mary the mother of

Jesus, and with his brethren" (Acts 1:14). The word "all" is the Greek word *pantes*, which describes *all of them*. It is *an all-encompassing word*, which indicates *no one was excluded*.

The word "continued" is also important. It is the Greek word *proskartereo*, and it means *to persevere consistently*. It pictures *intense focus and hard work; constant diligence and effort that never lets up*. This word depicts *one who is fixed in a forward position and is nearly addicted to what he or she is doing*. The use of this word tells us that when the disciples gathered in this room, they didn't just lounge around and wonder what was going to happen — they quickly began to *lean forward and press into prayer to obtain what Jesus had promised them*.

Acts 1:14 also says that the disciples were in "one accord," which in Greek is the word *homothumadon*; a compound of the words *homou* and *thumos*. The word *homou* points to *a moment when something happens at one time or simultaneously*; the word *thumos* depicts *passion*. When these words are compounded, the new word *homothumadon* pictures *those who are stirred up, excited, and are at one moment caught up in an eruption of passion*. This tells us that as Jesus' disciples steadfastly pressed in to intense, focused prayer, all of them — no one excluded — experienced both high points and low points.

This brings us to the word "prayer," which is a translation of the Greek word *proseuche*. This is a *close, up-front, intimate contact*. It denotes *coming close to express a wish, desire, prayer, or vow*. Originally this word was used to depict *a person who vowed to give something of great value to God in exchange for a favorable answer to prayer*. This is what the word "supplication" means and is why the translators included it in the *King James* text — even though it does not appear in the original Greek. Moreover, the word *proseuche* portrays *an individual who desires to see his prayer answered so desperately that he is willing to surrender everything he owns in exchange for answered prayer*. Hence, contained in this word is the concept of *surrender*.

So when the believers gathered in the Upper Room, they weren't gathering for a brief devotional, a few minutes of prayer, and some refreshments. They literally assembled to get as close to God as they possibly could. In that intimate position, they surrendered to His will and offered Him everything they had in exchange for the promised Gift of the Holy Spirit.

There Were 120 People in the Upper Room Including Mary, the Mother of Jesus, and His Brothers

Looking again at Acts 1:14, it says the disciples were praying "...with the women, and Mary the mother of Jesus, and with his brethren." The phrase "with the women" in Greek is *sun gunaixin*, which means *together with women* or *in partnership with women*. This demonstrates that in God's eyes, women are just as important as men and they were involved in ministry from the onset of the Church.

This Scripture also specifically notes that "Mary the mother of Jesus" was present, which is exactly what it means. It also says the disciples were praying "with his brethren." In Greek, this reads *kai sun tois adelphois autou*, and it literally means *together with his multiple natural brothers*. The word *sun* here implies *partnership*. Thus, Jesus' natural brothers were in *partnership* with what was taking place in that room.

Judas Had Abdicated His Divine Call to 'Ministry'

The Bible goes on to say, "And in those days Peter stood up in the midst of the disciples, and said, (the number of names together were about an hundred and twenty,) men and brethren, this scripture must needs have been fulfilled, which the Holy Ghost by the mouth of David spake before concerning Judas, which was guide to them that took Jesus" (Acts 1:15,16).

The word "guide" in verse 16 is the Greek word *hodegos*, and it describes *a guide who shows a traveler the safest course through an unknown country; one who knows all the paths, tracks, and roads*. Judas was called a "guide" because he was very familiar with Jesus and the places He frequently went to pray.

Peter continued, "For he [Judas] was numbered with us, and had obtained part of this ministry" (Acts 1:17). The word "numbered" is the Greek word *katarithmeo*, which is from the word *arithmetic*, and it means *counted* or *numbered among*. "With us" is from the Greek words *en hemin* which means *literally, in us; among us*. Peter was saying that Judas had been counted among the other disciples.

The word "obtained" is the Greek word *lagchano*, which means *to receive something by divine allotment*. Although Judas threw away his opportunity, the word *lagchano* clearly indicates that he had been divinely called by

God to be in ministry. The word "ministry" is the Greek word *diakonia*, from the word *diakonos*, and it describes *a high-level servant*. Historically, it depicted *sophisticated and highly trained servants who served the needs of others*. Thus, Jesus taught His disciples — including Judas — to be high-level, professional servants. They were trained to be the best they could be as they served the needs of others.

Furthermore, the word *diakonos* described *a waiter or waitress who painstakingly attended to the needs, wishes, and desires of his or her client*. The primary responsibility of such servants was to serve food and wait on tables. These were *servants who professionally pleased clients*. This was *a type of serving that was honorable, pleasurable, and done in a fashion that made people being served feel as if they were nobility*. Here in Acts 1:17, this word is used to depict *anyone in the ministry*, which includes us. We are to be the best we can be as we serve the needs of others.

Matthias Was Selected To Be a 'Witness' for Christ and So Are You

Keep in mind that this process of selecting a replacement for Judas was all taking place in Mary's large, upper-level living room in downtown Jerusalem. As the apostles continued to deliberate their decision, Peter added, "Wherefore of these men which have companied with us all the time that the Lord Jesus went in and out among us, beginning from the baptism of John, unto that same day that he was taken up from us, must one be ordained to be a witness with us of his resurrection" (Acts 1:21,22).

The word "witness" is the Greek word *martus*, and it describes *one summoned to testify in a court of law; a legal witness that was only allowed to speak what he personally knew to be true*. This word can also picture *the evidence presented in a legal case*. The word *martus* could be connected to the idea of suffering because one called to be a witness was required to be faithful to the truth, regardless of any possible acts of retribution that might be carried out against him by those who opposed his witness or wished to suppress the truth. When summoned to be a witness, it was inherently understood that this act could place an individual or his loved ones in jeopardy. Thus, *to be a witness required the highest level of integrity and commitment, as well as a willingness to sacrifice oneself or one's status to uphold the truth*.

Once the criteria for being a witness was given, the Bible says, "...they appointed two, Joseph called Barsabas, who was surnamed Justus, and Matthias. And they prayed, and said, Thou, Lord, which knowest the hearts of all men, shew whether of these two thou hast chosen" (Acts 1:23,24).

The phrase "knowest the hearts" in Greek is the word *kardiognostes*, a compound of the word *kardia* and the word *gnostes*. The word *kardia* depicts *the heart or the innermost part of a person*; the word *gnostes* means *to know like an expert*. When these two words are joined to form *kardiognostes*, it would literally be translated *the heart-knower* or *the expert of all human hearts*. That is exactly who Jesus is.

As the apostles prayed, they said, "Thou, Lord," which is a translation of the Greek words *Su Kurie*, The word *su* implies *intimacy and direct speech*; the word *Kurie* is the direct form of *kurios*, meaning *lord or supreme master*. This address indicates that the apostles were pressing into the presence of the Lord and speaking directly to Him. In these words are both *intimacy* and *respect*.

The word "chosen" is from the Greek word *eklego*, which means *to say out*. It is the equivalent of saying, "Which one of these men have You already spoken their name? To which one have You already extended and confirmed Your call?"

Acts 1:26 goes on to say, "And they gave forth their lots; and the lot fell upon Matthias; and he was numbered with the eleven apostles." In Greek, the phrase "gave forth their lots" is a picture of *a game of dice*. At that moment, none of the apostles had been baptized in the Holy Spirit. The best they could do to make the right decision concerning Judas' replacement was to cast the dice and pray for the right answer. God helped them in their seeking, the dice rolled in favor of Matthias, and he was numbered with the eleven to serve as a witness for Christ from then on.

STUDY QUESTIONS

> Study to shew thyself approved unto God, a workman that needeth
> not to be ashamed, rightly dividing the word of truth.
> — 2 Timothy 2:15

The Early Church understood the transforming power of prayer. James 5:16 (*AMPC*) says, "…The earnest (heartfelt, continued) prayer of a righteous man makes tremendous power available [dynamic in its working]."

1. According to John 15:7 and Jeremiah 23:28, what should your prayers include? (Also consider Isaiah 62:6 in the Amplified Bible.)
2. When God hears you include this in your prayers, how does He respond (consider Jeremiah 1:12; Psalm 103:20; and Numbers 23:19).
3. How do Jesus' words in John 14:12-14 and John's words in First John 5:14 and 15 give you hope and confidence that God will hear and answer your prayers?

PRACTICAL APPLICATION

But be ye doers of the word, and not hearers only,
deceiving your own selves.
—James 1:22

The Bible says all the disciples "continued" in prayer. In Greek, the word "continued" is *proskartereo*, which means *to persevere consistently*. It pictures *intense focus, hard work, and constant diligence and effort that never lets up.*

1. Can you remember a time in your life when you "continued" in prayer? What were you intensely focused on and persevering in prayer about? Did you receive what you were seeking?
2. Is there anything you need to "continue" in prayer about right now? What is it? Take time now to press in and seek the face of God for His provision and intervention in your situation.

TOPIC

How Would You Like To Have Pentecost in Your Living Room?

SCRIPTURES

1. **Acts 1:12-14** — Then returned they unto Jerusalem from the mount called Olivet, which is from Jerusalem a sabbath day's journey. And when they were come in, they went up into an upper room, where abode both Peter, and James, and John, and Andrew, Philip, and Thomas, Bartholomew, and Matthew, James the son of Alphaeus, and Simon Zelotes, and Judas the brother of James. These all continued with one accord in prayer and supplication, with the women, and Mary the mother of Jesus, and with his brethren.

2. **Acts 2:1-4** — And when the day of Pentecost was fully come, they were all with one accord in one place. And suddenly there came a sound from heaven as of a rushing mighty wind, and it filled all the house where they were sitting. And there appeared unto them cloven tongues like as of fire, and it sat upon each of them. And they were all filled with the Holy Ghost, and began to speak with other tongues, as the Spirit gave them utterance.

GREEK WORDS

1. "upper room" — ὑπερῷον (*huperoon*): the highest part of the house; the upper rooms or upper story of a house; a room in the upper part of a house; upper chamber; usually the largest open space in an ancient home

2. "abode" — καταμένω (*katameno*): to settle down and stay; to remain consistently

3. "all" — πάντες (*pantes*) all of them; an all-encompassing word; no one was excluded

4. "continued" — προσκαρτερέω (*proskartereo*): to persevere consistently; pictures intense focus and hard work; constant diligence

and effort that never lets up; pictures one who is fixed in a forward position

5. "one accord" — ὁμοθυμαδόν (*homothumadon*): a compound of ὁμοῦ (*homou*) and θυμός (*thumos*); the word ὁμοῦ (*homou*) points to a moment when something happens at one time or simultaneously; the word θυμός (*thumos*) pictures passion; compounded, pictures those who are stirred up, excited, and are at one moment caught up in an eruption of passion; a thrilling moment

6. "prayer" — προσευχή (*proseuche*): close, up-front, intimate contact; coming close to express a wish, desire, prayer, or vow; originally used to depict a person who vowed to give something of great value to God in exchange for a favorable answer to prayer; portrays an individual who desires to see his prayer answered so desperately that he is willing to surrender everything he owns in exchange for answered prayer; hence, contained in this word is the concept of surrender

7. "with the women" — σὺν γυναιξὶν (*sun gunaixin*): together with women; in partnership with women

8. "and Mary the mother of Jesus" — καὶ Μαριὰμ τῇ μητρὶ τοῦ Ἰησοῦ (*kai Mariam te metri tou Iesou*): literally, "and Mary the mother of Jesus"

9. "and with his brethren" — καὶ σὺν τοῖς ἀδελφοῖς αὐτοῦ (*kai sun tois adelphois autou*): and together with his multiple natural brothers; the word σύν (*sun*) implies partnership with his brothers

10. PENTECOST — πεντηκοστή (*pentekoste*): fiftieth day after Passover; Pentecost, the second of three great Jewish feasts

11. "one accord" — ὁμοῦ (*homou*): together; in one place

12. "in one place" — ἐπὶ τὸ αὐτό (*epi to auto*): upon the place; gathered in one spot; literally, in the one [place]

13. "suddenly there came" — ἐγένετο ἄφνω (*egeneto aphno*): the word ἐγένετο (*enegeto*), a form of γίνομαι (*ginomai*), depicts something that takes one off guard or by surprise; the word ἄφνω (*aphno*) means suddenly or unexpectedly; as a phrase, something happened that took them completely off guard and by surprise

14. "sound" — ἦχος (*echos*): the same word describes the violent roaring and overwhelming sound of the sea in the middle of a huge storm

15. "from heaven" — ἐκ τοῦ οὐρανοῦ (*ek tou ouranou*): right out of heaven; directly out of heaven

16. "as of" — ὥσπερ (*hosper*): just as; like; exactly like
17. "rushing" — φερομένης (*pheromenes*): from φέρω (*phero*); being carried; being borne
18. "mighty" — βίαιος (*biaias*): forceful; mighty; violent
19. "wind" — πνοή (*pnoe*): blast; gust; wind; wind was often a symbol of God's powerful presence
20. "filled" — ἐπλήρωσεν (*eplerosen*): a form of πληρόω (*pleroo*), to make full; to fill completely; to fill to the point of satisfaction
21. "all" — ὅλος (*holos*): the whole house; no part of it was untouched
22. "appeared" — ὁράω (*horao*): to see; to delightfully view; to fully view
23. "tongues" — γλῶσσα (*glossa*): there were flame-like appearances
24. "fire" — πῦρ (*pur*): fire; fire is a symbol of the presence of God as early as Genesis 15:17
25. "sat" — καθίζω (*kathidzo*): to sit down; to settle; figuratively, to hover
26. "began to speak" — ἤρξαντο λαλεῖν (*erdzanto lalein*): "I speak"; implies initiative; this involved their own initiative and participation; they commenced to speak; they commenced to converse
27. "other" — ἕτερος (*heteros*): a different kind; another of a different kind, as opposed to one that is familiar or similar
28. "gave" — ἐδίδου (*edidou*): from δίδωμι (*didomi*), which means to give, to impart, or to transfer
29. "them" — αὐτοῖς (*autois*): to them; he gave to them this divine ability; the Spirit gave, imparted, or transferred to them; emphasis is on them

SYNOPSIS

In the year 70 AD, the Upper Room in Jerusalem was destroyed by Rome's invasion. It was reconstructed by believers a few decades later during the reign of Emperor Hadrian and put back into use. Around 614 AD, it was demolished again when the Persians invaded and began occupying Jerusalem. Hundreds of years later, in the Twelfth Century, this holy site was rebuilt and enhanced by the crusaders. The last modifications made to the Upper Room took place in the Fourteenth Century. Hence, it has remained architecturally untouched for nearly 800 years. Historians agree it is the authentic place where a plethora of biblical events took place — including the unprecedented outpouring of the Holy Spirit on the Day of Pentecost.

The emphasis of this lesson:

When you fully surrender your home and life to Jesus, you too can experience the power of Pentecost. Your marriage, your children, and your entire family will be filled with the mighty presence of the Holy Spirit.

After Jesus ascended into Heaven, the Bible says, "Then returned they [the disciples] unto Jerusalem from the mount called Olivet, which is from Jerusalem a sabbath day's journey. And when they were come in, they went up into an upper room, where abode both Peter, and James, and John, and Andrew, Philip, and Thomas, Bartholomew, and Matthew, James the son of Alphaeus, and Simon Zelotes, and Judas the brother of James" (Acts 1:12,13).

Remember, Jesus had instructed His disciples not to depart from Jerusalem but to wait for the promised gift of the Holy Spirit (*see* Acts 1:4,5). In obedience, they returned to the city and made their way into the upper room of a familiar home where they had spent countless hours and days with Jesus. This room was in Mary's house — a wealthy widow who lived near the Temple Mount in the central district of Jerusalem. Mary was the mother of John Mark, who later became Peter's secretary and wrote the gospel of Mark. She was also the sister of Barnabas whose name means "son of encouragement." Barnabas was Paul's traveling companion on his first missionary journey.

The words "upper room" in Acts 1:13 is the Greek word *huperoon*, which describes *the highest part of the house; the upper rooms or upper story of a house*. It was usually *the largest open space in an ancient home*. In this case, the Upper Room was *the upper chamber* in Mary's home located on the second or third floor. Rooms like these were commonplace in the First Century and served as the first churches. This was where the disciples gathered as they waited in Jerusalem.

All the Disciples Continued in One Accord in Prayer

Acts 1:14 says, "These all continued with one accord in prayer and supplication, with the women, and Mary the mother of Jesus, and with his brethren." We saw that the word "all" here is the Greek word *pantes*, which means *all of them*. It is *an all-encompassing word*, which indicates *no one was excluded*. All 120 people assembled were personally involved with what was happening.

The word "continued" is also significant. It is the Greek word *proskartereo*, which means *to persevere consistently*. It pictures *intense focus and hard work; constant diligence and effort that never lets up*. The use of this word depicts the disciples *fixed in a forward position, pressing in to receive what Jesus said was coming*. This was their sole purpose, and they were nearly addicted to seeing it happen.

Additionally, the Scripture says the disciples were in "one accord," which in Greek is the word *homothumadon*. It is a compound of the word *homou*, which points to *a moment when something happens at one time or simultaneously*; and the word *thumos*, which pictures *passion*. When these words are joined, the new word *homothumadon* pictures *those who are stirred up, excited, and are at one moment caught up in an eruption of passion*. They were experiencing a preview of what was coming.

What were these faithful followers of Christ doing? The Bible says they continued in "prayer," which is the Greek word *proseuche*. This word describes *a close, up-front, intimate contact*. It denotes *coming close to express a wish, desire, prayer, or vow*. Originally, this word was used to depict *a person who vowed to give something of great value to God in exchange for a favorable answer to prayer*. It portrays *an individual who desires to see his prayer answered so desperately that he is willing to surrender everything he owns in exchange for answered prayer*. Hence, prayer (*proseuche*) contains the idea of *surrender*. Essentially, the disciples were saying, "God, we'll give you all that we are and all that we have if you will give us all of You."

Jesus' Mother and Brothers Spoke in Tongues

Something else important to note is that the disciples were praying "… with the women, and Mary the mother of Jesus, and with his brethren" (Acts 1:14). The phrase "with the women" in Greek is *sun gunaixin*, which means *together with women* or *in partnership with women*. This was truly a miracle of God. Normally, women were not allowed to participate in such spiritual gatherings. However, when God began building His Church, He chose women, signifying that in His eyes, women are just as important as men.

One woman specifically mentioned in Scripture who was in the Upper Room was "Mary the mother of Jesus." The Bible then adds the phrase "and with his brethren," which in Greek is *kai sun tois adelphois autou*, which literally means *together with his multiple natural brothers*. Thus, the disciples were praying with Mary the mother of Jesus as well as Jesus' biological brothers. At that point in time, Jesus' natural brothers were in *partnership* with what He was doing. No longer did they see Him as mentally unstable. Even James, who had been Jesus' adversary during much of His earthly ministry, was now living in full support of his eldest brother.

So if Mary the mother of Jesus and the natural-born brothers of Jesus were present in the Upper Room on the Day of Pentecost, it means that they too were baptized in the Holy Spirit and spoke in tongues! They fully embraced the Pentecostal experience and flowed in the gifts of the Spirit.

The Upper Room Was Ground Zero On the Day of Pentecost

Acts 2 documents one of the most powerful moments in the history of the world. The Bible says, "And when the day of Pentecost was fully come, they were all with one accord in one place" (Acts 2:1). The word "Pentecost" here means *the fiftieth day after Passover*. Pentecost was the second of three great Jewish feasts. Thus, Pentecost is not just the name of a modern-day denomination or a certain sect of Christians. It is a word marking the fiftieth day after Passover, which was the final day of the Festival of Weeks.

On that day, the Bible says the 120 that were gathered in the Upper Room "...were all with one accord in one place" (Acts 2:1). The word "all" is again the Greek word *pantes*, which indicates *all of them; no one was excluded*. The phrase "one accord" means *together* or *in one place*. And "one place," the Greek words *epi to auto*, depicts *being gathered together in one spot*. There is something truly powerful about God's people coming together in one place and praying together in unity

The Bible goes on to say, "And suddenly there came a sound from heaven as of a rushing mighty wind, and it filled all the house where they were sitting" (Acts 2:2). Notice the phrase "suddenly there came," which in Greek is *egeneto aphno*. The word *enegeto*, a form of the word *ginomai*, depicts *something that takes one off guard or by surprise*; the word *aphno* means *suddenly* or *unexpectedly*. When these words come together as a phrase, it means *something happened that took them completely off guard and by surprise*.

These men and women of God had been praying intensely for about ten days to receive the gift of the Holy Spirit. Ironically, when the Spirit finally came, they were completely caught off guard because what occurred was not what they expected.

'There Came a Sound from Heaven'

The Bible says, "…there came a sound from heaven… (Acts 2:2)." The word "sound" in Greek is *echos*, which is the same word used to describe *the violent roaring and overwhelming sound of the sea in the middle of a huge storm*. The words "from heaven" in Greek is *ek tou ouranou*, which means *right out of heaven* or *directly out of heaven*. This violent, roaring sound came directly out of Heaven and pierced the atmosphere of the Upper Room. Heaven was invading Mary's home.

The sound from Heaven was "…as of a rushing mighty wind…." In Greek, the words "as of" is *hosper*, which means *just as*; *like*; or *exactly like*. The sound from Heaven was *exactly like* a "rushing mighty wind." The word "rushing" is *pheromones* in Greek, which is from the word *phero*, and it means *being carried* or *being borne*. The word "mighty" is the Greek word *biaias*, and it describes *something forceful, mighty, or violent*. And the word "wind" is the Greek word *pnoe*, which describes *a real blast or gust of wind*. Throughout Scripture, wind was often a symbol of God's powerful presence.

Take a moment to imagine what was actually taking place. One hundred and twenty devoted believers were passionately united in prayer in the large second or third story room of Mary's home in the center of Jerusalem. They had been pressing in and praying for several days, when all of a sudden God moved! The spirit world invaded the natural world with a sound so forceful and fierce it must have been deafening.

In that moment, the rushing mighty wind "filled all the house." The word "filled" is the Greek word *eplesthesan*, which is a form of *pleroo*, and it means *to make full, to fill completely*; or *to fill to the point of satisfaction*. The word "all" here is the Greek word *holos*, and it denotes *the whole house; no part of it was untouched*. Thus, every nook and cranny of every room of the house was filled with the powerful manifestation of God's Spirit.

'There Appeared Unto Them Cloven Tongues of Fire'

Acts 2:3 goes on to say, "And there appeared unto them cloven tongues like as of fire, and it sat upon each of them." The word "appeared" in this verse is a form of the Greek word *horao*, which means *to see*; *to delightfully view*; or *to fully view*. The use of this word tells us that those in attendance could physically see something taking place before their very eyes, and they were delighted by it.

The Bible states that "cloven tongues like as of fire" is what appeared in plain sight. The word "cloven" means *divided*. The word "tongues" is the Greek word *glossa*, and it indicates *there were flame-like appearances of "fire."* The word "fire" in Greek is *pur*, and has been a symbol of the presence of God since He cut covenant with Abraham in Genesis 15:17. In Scripture, fire *purifies*, *brings illumination*, *provides warmth and life, and it produces energy and power*.

Suddenly, out of nowhere, the fire of God materialized in the atmosphere of the room and began to divide in what appeared to be tongue-like flames that "sat upon each of them." The word "sat" in Greek is *kathidzo*, which means *figuratively to hover, sit down, or to settle on each of them*.

All Were Filled with the Holy Spirit

Acts 2:4 says. "And they were all filled with the Holy Ghost...." The word "all" is again the Greek word *pantes*, which is an all-inclusive word indicating *all of them; no one was excluded* from being "filled." The word "filled" is a form of the Greek word *pleroo*, meaning *to make full, to fill completely*.

When the disciples were filled, the Bible says they "began to speak," which in Greek is *erdzanto lulein*, and it carries the idea of *initiative*. Hence, the disciples *involved their own initiative and participation and they commenced to speak and to converse* in "other tongues." The word "other" is the Greek word *heteros*, which means *another of a different kind, as opposed to one that is familiar or similar*. What they spoke was not a language with which they were familiar.

The Bible says the disciples spoke "...as the Spirit gave them utterance." The word "gave" is the Greek word *edidou*, from the word *didomi*, which means *to give, to impart, or to transfer*. And the word "them" in Greek is *autois*, which means *to them; the Spirit gave, imparted, or transferred to them this divine ability*, and the emphasis is on them.

A careful study of the book of Acts reveals that every time the Holy Spirit filled people, they spoke with other tongues. This is a definitive pattern revealed in Acts chapters 2, 8, 9 10, and 19. The Holy Spirit imparted, or transferred, to each recipient the divine ability to speak in a different kind of tongue than with what they were familiar.

STUDY QUESTIONS

Study to shew thyself approved unto God, a workman that needeth not to be ashamed, rightly dividing the word of truth.
— 2 Timothy 2:15

1. What new insights did you discover about the Day of Pentecost that you had not seen previously? Did you know that Mary the mother of Jesus and His brothers were there? What does this speak to you personally about the baptism in the Holy Spirit and speaking in tongues?
2. According to Acts 2:38 and 39, who is the Baptism in the Holy Spirit for, and what must one do to receive this? (Also consider Jesus' words in Luke 11:9-13.)
3. Praying in the heavenly prayer language of the spirit is truly life-giving. What do Jude 20 and First Corinthians 14:4 say will happen when we pray in the spirit? Why is praying in the spirit so beneficial when you're overwhelmed and don't know how to pray? (*See* Romans 8:26,27.)

PRACTICAL APPLICATION

But be ye doers of the word, and not hearers only, deceiving your own selves.
— James 1:22

1. When God began building His Church, He specifically chose women, signifying that in His eyes, women are equally important as men. How do you view the involvement of men and women in the Church? Is there anything you feel is off limits to either sex? If so, what is it and why do you feel this way?
2. The events that took place on the Day of Pentecost described in Acts 2 are not figurative — they are literal. The spirit world invaded the physical world, and the power of the Holy Spirit violently shook the place and filled the people. Have you ever experienced a time when

the Holy Spirit physically manifested with such magnitude? If so, describe what took place? How was your life and the lives of those in attendance forever impacted?

TOPIC

Jesus Wants To Rendezvous in Your Living Room

SCRIPTURES

1. **Acts 4:23-31** — And being let go, they went to their own company, and reported all that the chief priests and elders had said unto them. And when they heard that, they lifted up their voice to God with one accord, and said, Lord, thou art God, which hast made heaven, and earth, and the sea, and all that in them is: Who by the mouth of thy servant David hast said, Why did the heathen rage, and the people imagine vain things? The kings of the earth stood up, and the rulers were gathered together against the Lord, and against his Christ. For of a truth against thy holy child Jesus, whom thou hast anointed, both Herod, and Pontius Pilate, with the Gentiles, and the people of Israel, were gathered together, for to do whatsoever thy hand and thy counsel determined before to be done. And now, Lord, behold their threatenings: and grant unto thy servants, that with all boldness they may speak thy word, by stretching forth thine hand to heal; and that signs and wonders may be done by the name of thy holy child Jesus. And when they had prayed, the place was shaken where they were assembled together; and they were all filled with the Holy Ghost, and they spake the word of God with boldness.

GREEK WORDS

1. "let go" — ἀπολύω (*apoluo*): being untied and unloose, they were dismissed and released to go

2. "own company" — ἰδίους (*idious*): plural form of ἴδιος (*idios*); uniquely their own; to their own group; to their own community; to those who were like them

3. "reported" — ἀπαγγέλλω (*apangello*): the word ἀπό (*apo*) and **aggello** (*angello*); the word ἀπό (*apo*) means back and **aggello** (*angello*) means to report; to report back; to give a full report, giving a sense of duty to fully report back to their own about all that had happened and all that had been said to them; implies a sense of responsibility to report back to their own

4. "lifted up" — αἴρω (*airo*): to lift up; to raise up; to elevate

5. "voice" — φωνή (*phone*): voice; sound; depicts something noisy

6. "one accord" — ὁμοθυμαδόν (*homothumadon*): a compound of ὁμοῦ (*homou*) and θυμός (*thumos*); the word ὁμοῦ (*homou*) points to a moment when something happens at one time or simultaneously; the word θυμός (*thumos*) pictures passion; compounded, pictures those who are stirred up, excited, and are at one moment caught up in an eruption of passion; a thrilling moment

7. "Lord" — Δέσποτα (*Despota*): direct form of δεσπότης (*despotes*); master; an authority figure who exercises complete jurisdiction; one who has unrestricted power, absolute domination, and who knows no limitations or restraints

8. "now" — νῦν (*nun*): right now; in this very moment; in this instant; exactly right now

9. "Lord" — Κύριε (*Kurie*): direct form of κύριος (*kurios*), meaning lord or supreme master

10. "behold" — ἐπεῖδεν (*epeiden*): look upon; open your eyes to behold; to comprehend; see

11. "threatenings" — ἀπειλή (*apeile*): menacing threats; menacing restrictions

12. "grant" — δίδωμι (*didomi*): to give, to impart, or to transfer

13. "thy" — σου (*sou*): personal pronoun; belonging to you; that are yours

14. "servants" — δοῦλος (*doulos*): one bound to do the bidding of his owner; a slave who is to help, assist, and fulfill his master's wants and dreams to the exclusion of all else; one whose will is completely swallowed up in the will of another

15. "boldness" — παρρησία (*parresia*): bold, frank, forthright speech; confidence; audacious; emboldened; extraordinarily frank; a daring

to speak what one believes or thinks, even in the face of retribution; unashamed confidence; frankness of speech that accompanies unflinching authority

16. "speak" — λαλέω (*laleo*): to freely speak; to freely converse; to fluently communicate; normal, unaffected speech

17. "thy word" — τὸν λόγον σου (*ton logon sou*): the Word of you; the Word originating with you; the Word coming from you; your Word; the definite article clearly means THE WORD

18. "by" — ἐν τῷ (*en to*): in that

19. "stretching forth" — ἐκτείνω (*ekteino*): to stretch forth; to reach out; to put down an anchor

20. "thine hand" — τὴν χεῖρά ‹σου› (*ten cheira 'sou'*): with a definite article, the hand of yours; specifically, your hand; conveys a sense of awe about THE HAND of God; the word hand, χεῖρά (*cheria*), figuratively depicts the power of God in the Old Testament

21. "to" — εἰς (*eis*): into; leading to; resulting in

22. "by" — διά (*dia*): through; implies agency and instrumentality

23. "prayed" — δέομαι (*deomai*): from δέησις (*deisis*); request for a concrete, specific need to be met, usually some type of physical or material need; a petition

24. "the place" — ὁ τόπος (*ho topos*): the specific place; the specific spot; the specific location

25. "shaken" — σαλεύω (*saleu*): to shake, waver, totter, to be moved; a state of alarm, distress, excitement, panic, or shock

26. "filled" — ἐπλήσθησαν (*eplesthesan*): a form of πληρόω (*pleroo*), to make full, to fill completely; to fill to the point of satisfaction

27. "spake" — λαλέω (*laleo*): to freely speak; to freely converse; to fluently communicate; normal, unaffected speech

28. "the word of God" — τὸν λόγον τοῦ Θεοῦ (*ton logon tou Theou*): definite article, meaning THE word of God, or THE word from God, or THE word originating in God

SYNOPSIS

Thus far we have seen how early in the First Century, a widow woman named Mary opened the doors of her home and made it available to Jesus and His disciples whenever they were in Jerusalem. Her large *upper room* became their rendezvous point during Jesus' ministry and continued to serve as a meeting place for believers in the Early Church for decades afterwards.

Today, over 2,000 years later, devoted Christians from all over the world still journey to this sacred space to experience the presence of God and remember the many events that took place here during Christ's life and after He ascended into Heaven — including the Holy Ghost's worldwide invasion on the Day of Pentecost. Again and again, believers in the Early Church were filled and refilled with a fresh anointing of the Holy Spirit to boldly speak God's Word and bring forth signs and wonders in His Name.

The emphasis of this lesson:

There is one Baptism in the Holy Spirit, but there are many infillings that take place in a believer's life. The Early Church experienced the initial outpouring of the Holy Spirit on the Day of Pentecost. Yet, they were refilled again and again as they continued to seek the Lord.

In Acts chapter 3, we find Peter and John going to the temple for the hour of prayer, and while they were on their way, they met a lame man who had been crippled from birth. When they locked eyes on him, the man expected and prepared to receive something. "Then Peter said, Silver and gold have I none; but such as I have give I thee: In the name of Jesus Christ of Nazareth rise up and walk" (Acts 3:6). Immediately, the power of God was released through their prayer, and the man was healed.

Word of his amazing healing quickly spread among the people at the temple. They knew who this man was and had seen him sitting and begging at the Beautiful gate for years. Now he was walking and leaping and praising God. In the atmosphere of awe and wonder, Peter seized the opportunity and began preaching the Good News of Jesus to all who would listen, urging them to repent and receive Christ into their lives.

When the Sadducees, the priests, and the captain of the temple heard that Peter and John were teaching about Jesus, the Bible says, "they laid hands on them, and put them in hold unto the next day..." (Acts 4:3). In the morning, the disciples were brought before Caiaphas the high priest and many other Jewish leaders and asked, "...By what power, or by what name, have ye done this?" (Acts 4:7.) The original Greek text in verse 8 reveals that in that moment, Peter and John were instantaneously refilled with the Holy Spirit and began to speak the Word boldly.

Peter and John Returned to Their 'Own Company'

After many threats, the Jewish leaders released the disciples, and the Bible says, "And being let go, they went to their own company, and reported all that the chief priests and elders had said unto them" (Acts 4:23). Let's unpack the meaning of a few key words in this verse, starting with the phrase "let go." It is the Greek word *apoluo*, and it means *being untied and unloosed*. Peter and John *were dismissed and released to go*.

Also notice the words "own company." In Greek, this is the word *idious*, which is the plural form of *idios*, and it means *uniquely their own; to their own group; to their own community; to those who were like them*. Peter and John knew immediately where they needed to go — to the companions who shared their passionate devotion to Jesus.

When they arrived, the Bible says they "reported" all that happened. The word "reported" is the Greek word *apangello*, which is from the word *apo*, meaning *back*, and the word *aggello* (*angello*), meaning *to report*. When these two words are compounded to form the word *apangello*, it means *giving a sense of duty to fully report back to their own about all that had happened and all that had been said to them*. This word implies *a sense of responsibility to report back to their own*.

The Disciples Entered Into Corporate Prayer

It is interesting to note the place where Peter and John regrouped with the disciples to recount what had happened — the Upper Room of Mary's home. Acts 4:24 goes on to say, "And when they [the disciples] heard that, they lifted up their voice to God with one accord...." The phrase "lifted up" in Greek is *airo*, which means *to lift up; to raise up*; or *to elevate*. And the word "voice" is the Greek word *phone*, which describes *one's voice* or *a sound*; it can also depict *something noisy*.

Thus, when all the followers of Jesus who were gathered in the Upper Room heard Peter and John's report, they immediately entered in to corporate prayer, lifting their voice to God. Although there were many people praying, what may have sounded like confusion to the natural ears, in God's ears He heard one united voice coming from the hearts of His people.

The Bible says they were praying in "one accord," which is again the Greek word *homothumadon*. It is a compound of the word *homou*, which *points to a moment when something happens at one time or simultaneously*, and the word *thumos*, which pictures *passion*. When these words are compounded, the word *homothumadon* pictures *those who are stirred up, excited, and are at one moment caught up in an eruption of passion*; it is *a thrilling moment*.

This word shows us the power of corporate prayer. When a group or church prays together in tongues — each person lifting up his or her own voice in the language of the spirit — the prayers mix together and ascend into the ears of God in Heaven, and He hears one, single corporate prayer.

They Appealed Directly to the Lord

Notice how the early saints began their prayer: "…Lord, thou art God… (Acts 4:24). The word "Lord" here is very important. It is the Greek word *Despota*, which is a direct form of the word *despotes*, meaning *master*. It denotes *an authority figure who exercises complete jurisdiction; one who has unrestricted power, absolute domination, and who knows no limitations or restraints*. Hence, the disciples were looking at God as the All-Sufficient One who has absolute jurisdiction over everything.

They said, "…Lord, thou art God, which hast made heaven, and earth, and the sea, and all that in them is: Who by the mouth of thy servant David hast said, Why did the heathen rage, and the people imagine vain things? The kings of the earth stood up, and the rulers were gathered together against the Lord, and against his Christ. For of a truth against thy holy child Jesus, whom thou hast anointed, both Herod, and Pontius Pilate, with the Gentiles, and the people of Israel, were gathered together, for to do whatsoever thy hand and thy counsel determined before to be done" (Acts 4:24-28).

With one voice, the people of God began to corporately pray the Scriptures aloud — the Holy Spirit fueling the fire of their prayers. Then in Acts 4:29, the focus of their prayers shifted. They began to pour out their hearts and petition God saying, "And now, Lord, behold their threatenings: and grant unto thy servants, that with all boldness they may speak thy word."

The word "now" in this verse is the Greek word *nun*, which literally means *right now; in this very moment; in this instant; exactly right now*. Again, we see the word "Lord," but this time it is the Greek word *Kurie*, a direct form of *kurios*, meaning *lord* or *supreme master*. Because it is a direct form of *kurios*, it indicates that they are getting very personal with God and appealing to Him directly.

They said, "...Behold their threatenings..." (Acts 4:29). The word "behold" here is the Greek word *epeiden*, which means *look upon; open your eyes to behold; to comprehend; or see*. The word "threatenings" is *apeile* in Greek, and it describes *menacing threats* or *menacing restrictions*. The believers were directly appealing to God asking Him to open His eyes and see the menacing threats and restrictions the Jewish leaders were speaking to them. Specifically, the Jewish leaders had commanded the disciples not to speak or teach in the name of Jesus (*see* Acts 4:18).

The disciples continued their prayer saying, "...Grant unto thy servants, that with all boldness they may speak thy word" (Acts 4:29). The word "grant" here is a form of the Greek word *didomi*, which means *to give, to impart, or to transfer.* "Thy" is the Greek word *sou*, which is a personal pronoun meaning *belonging to you; that are yours*. And the word "servants" is a form of the Greek word *doulos*, which describes *one bound to do the bidding of his owner; a slave who is to help, assist, and fulfill his master's wants and dreams to the exclusion of all else*. It indicates *one whose will is completely swallowed up in the will of another*. Thus, when the believers said, "grant unto thy servants," they were literally saying, "Impart or transfer unto us, Your very own dedicated servants, what we need."

They Asked God for 'Boldness' To Speak His Word

The word "boldness" in Acts 4:29 is the Greek word *parresia*. It describes *bold, frank, forthright speech*. This word is sometimes translated as *confidence*. It depicts *someone audacious, emboldened, or extraordinarily frank*; it is *daring to speak what one believes or thinks, even in the face of retribution*. Moreover, it signifies *unashamed confidence* or *frankness of speech that accompanies unflinching authority*.

These Early Christians made a direct appeal to the Lord for boldness to "speak" His Word. The word "speak" here is the Greek word *laleo*, and it means *to freely speak; to freely converse*; or *to fluently communicate*. It describes *normal, unaffected speech*. They wanted the ability to freely and fluently communicate God's Word unashamedly and unflinchingly.

This brings us to the phrase "thy word," which in Greek is *ton logon sou*, and it literally means *the Word of you; the Word originating with you; the Word coming from you; your Word*. It includes the definite article, which clearly means THE WORD. The use of this language tells us that these believers were not going around sharing inspirational stories or telling jokes. They were preaching the Holy Scriptures, and as a result, God was showing up in unprecedented ways.

They Wanted Him To Manifest Signs and Wonders

In Acts 4:30, the disciples specifically requested the method by which they wanted the Lord to act. They said, "By stretching forth thine hand to heal; and that signs and wonders may be done by the name of thy holy child Jesus."

The phrase "stretching forth" is a translation of the Greek word *ekteino*, which means *to stretch forth* or *to reach out*. It was the same word used in the navigational world that meant *to put down an anchor*. This was the equivalent of saying, "Lord, we want You to drop Your anchor among us, extend thine hand, and begin to heal."

In Greek, "thine hand" is *ten cheira 'sou.'* It has a definite article, which means *the hand of yours*, or specifically, *your hand*. This word *conveys a sense of awe about THE HAND of God*. Moreover, the word "hand," which is the Greek word *cheria*, figuratively depicts *the power of God in the Old Testament*.

Even the word "to" is important. The believers prayed for God to stretch forth His mighty hand "to heal." The word "to" is the Greek word *eis*, and it would better be translated *leading to* or *resulting in healing*. When the hand of God manifests, supernatural things take place. So in addition to boldness to fluently speak the Scriptures, the disciples asked for signs and wonders to be done through the agency of the exalted name of Jesus.

God Answered the Disciples' Prayer

Acts 4:31 says, "And when they had prayed, the place was shaken where they were assembled together; and they were all filled with the Holy Ghost, and they spake the word of God with boldness." The word "prayed" here is the Greek word *deomai*, which is from the word *deisis*. It is *a request for a concrete, specific need to be met, usually some type of physical or material need; a petition.*

Once the people had presented their specific need to God the Bible says, "the place was shaken." In Greek, "the place" is *ho topos*, and it describes *the specific place; the specific spot; the specific location.* The word *topos* denotes *a geographical place*; it is from where we get the word for a *topographical map.* Thus, when the disciples finished giving God their petition, the Upper Room in Mary's home was "shaken."

"Shaken" is the Greek word *saleu,* and it means *to shake, waver, totter, or to be moved.* It depicts *a state of alarm, distress, excitement, panic, or shock.* As the building was physically shaking, the people became alarmed by what they were experiencing. Then suddenly, they were all "…filled with the Holy Ghost…." The word "filled" in Greek is *eplesthesan,* a form of *pleroo,* which means *to make full, to fill completely; to fill to the point of satisfaction.*

Furthermore, with this fresh infilling the Bible says, "…They spake the word of God with boldness" (Acts 4:31). The word "spake" is again the Greek word *laleo,* meaning *to freely speak; to freely converse; to fluently communicate.* In that instant, the disciples received specifically what they had prayed for. All the restrictions were removed from their speech, and they began to freely communicate "the Word of God" — which in Greek indicates *THE word originating in God.* And they spoke it with "boldness," which is the Greek word *parresia,* describing *bold, frank, forthright speech.*

Friend, God wants to fill you with His Holy Spirit so you can fluently speak and communicate His Word with boldness! He wants to give you a supernatural confidence and embolden you in such a way that you unashamedly dare to speak what you believe and think — even in the face of retribution. If you want this holy, unashamed confidence accompanied by unflinching authority, begin to seek God for it in prayer.

STUDY QUESTIONS

> Study to shew thyself approved unto God, a workman that needeth not to be ashamed, rightly dividing the word of truth.
> — 2 Timothy 2:15

1. Have you ever been afraid of speaking to others about Jesus? Many of us face this fear but Jesus doesn't want us to be anxious or worry about it. Check out what He says in Luke 12:11 and 12, and in your own words write out His amazing promise to you. (*See also* Matthew 10:19,20 and Mark 13:11.)

2. Believers in the Early Church asked God for boldness to speak His Word. In Jeremiah 23:28 (*AMPC*) God said, "…he who has My word,

let him speak My word faithfully...." What kind of results can you expect to happen when you faithfully speak the Word of God over your life, over your family, and to others? (*Read* Hebrews 4:12; James 1:21; Jeremiah 23:29.)

PRACTICAL APPLICATION

But be ye doers of the word, and not hearers only,
deceiving your own selves.
—James 1:22

1. When Peter and John were released from their interrogation by the Jewish leaders, the Bible says they returned to "their own company"— those with whom they did life and shared the same faith. Who would you say is your "own company"? If you had just experienced a trying time as Peter and John did, to whom would you share it?

2. The time of prayer that took place in the Upper Room in Acts 4 is an example of what happens when the Church comes together in corporate prayer. Have you ever experienced the manifestation of the Holy Spirit during corporate prayer? If so, share what happened. Who can you begin to join together with on a regular basis and pray in the Spirit on behalf of your families, your city, and your nation?

3. As threats made by the Jewish rulers and scribes weighed upon the Church, believers took their menacing situation to the Lord in prayer. What situation is weighing heavily upon you? Take time right now to partner in prayer with someone you know and invite God to get involved. Remember, pray in the language of the spirit. The Holy Spirit will pray through you when you are weak and don't know what to pray (*see* Romans 8:26,27).

TOPIC
How Would You Like a Divine Visitation in Your Living Room?

SCRIPTURES

1. **Acts 12:1-17,19** — Now about that time Herod the king stretched forth his hands to vex certain of the church. And he killed James the brother of John with the sword. And because he saw it pleased the Jews, he proceeded further to take Peter also. (Then were the days of unleavened bread.) And when he had apprehended him, he put him in prison, and delivered him to four quaternions of soldiers to keep him; intending after Easter to bring him forth to the people. Peter therefore was kept in prison: but prayer was made without ceasing of the church unto God for him. And when Herod would have brought him forth, the same night Peter was sleeping between two soldiers, bound with two chains: and the keepers before the door kept the prison. And, behold, the angel of the Lord came upon him, and a light shined in the prison: and he smote Peter on the side, and raised him up, saying, Arise up quickly. And his chains fell off from his hands. And the angel said unto him, Gird thyself, and bind on thy sandals. And so he did. And he saith unto him, Cast thy garment about thee, and follow me. And he went out, and followed him; and wist not that it was true which was done by the angel; but thought he saw a vision. When they were past the first and the second ward, they came unto the iron gate that leadeth unto the city; which opened to them of his own accord: and they went out, and passed on through one street; and forthwith the angel departed from him. And when Peter was come to himself, he said, Now I know of a surety, that the Lord hath sent his angel, and hath delivered me out of the hand of Herod, and from all the expectation of the people of the Jews. And when he had considered the thing, he came to the house of Mary the mother of John, whose surname was Mark; where many were gathered together praying. And as Peter knocked at the door of the gate, a damsel came to hearken, named Rhoda. And when she knew Peter's voice, she opened not the gate for gladness, but ran in, and told how Peter

stood before the gate. And they said unto her, Thou art mad. But she constantly affirmed that it was even so. Then said they, It is his angel. But Peter continued knocking: and when they had opened the door, and saw him, they were astonished. But he, beckoning unto them with the hand to hold their peace, declared unto them how the Lord had brought him out of the prison. And he said, Go shew these things unto James, and to the brethren. And he departed, and went into another place.... And when Herod had sought for him, and found him not, he examined the keepers, and commanded that they should be put to death. And he went down from Judaea to Caesarea, and there abode.

GREEK WORDS

1. "stretched forth" — ἐπιβάλλω (*epiballo*): to lay his hand upon; to forcibly lay upon

2. "his hands" — τὰς χεῖρας (*tas cheiras*): plural, hands; indicating meddling

3. "vex" — κακόω (*kakao*): abuse; harm; injure; maltreat; mistreat

4. "church" — ἐκκλησία (*ekklesia*): a called, separated, and prestigious assembly; in history, denoted a prestigious assembly who determined laws, debated public policy, formulated new policies, and ruled in judicial matters; to be invited to this assembly was a great honor; the body of believers who have assembled to be God's representatives in every town, city, state, or nation; a body called to make decisions that affect the atmosphere of a region

5. "proceeded further" — προσέθετο (*prosetheto*): to proceed with a plan

6. "take" — συλλαμβάνω (*sullambano*): to conceive, as a pregnancy; a well-conceived plan to apprehend; a well-thought-out plan to apprehend; pictures a sting operation

7. "also" — καὶ (*kai*): also; even

8. "apprehended" — πιάζω (*piadzo*): to catch; to lay hold of; to seize

9. "four quaternions" — τέσσαρσιν τετραδίοις (*tessarsin tetradiois*): two soldiers were confined with the prisoner and two kept guard outside

10. "intending" — βούλομαι (*boulomai*): planning; to do something with counsel

11. "Easter" — πάσχα (*pascha*): Passover, not Easter

12. "kept" — **τηρέω** (*tereo*): pictures soldiers who were faithful to their charge of keeping watch regardless of assaults or the number of attackers they might encounter

13. "prayer" — **προσευχή** (*proseuche*): pictures close, up-front, intimate contact; coming close to express a wish, desire, prayer, or vow; used to depict a person who vowed to give something of great value to God in exchange for a favorable answer to prayer; it portrays an individual who desires to see his prayer answered so desperately that he is willing to surrender everything he owns in exchange for answered prayer; contained in this word is the concept of surrender

14. "without ceasing" — **ἐκτενῶς**: fervently; in an extended, stretched out manner; without let-up

15. "unto God" — **πρὸς τὸν Θεὸν** (*pros ton Theon*): face to face with God; see John 1:1

16. "sleeping" — **κοιμάομαι** (*koimaomai*): pictures sleep; a deep sleep; sometimes refers to the sleep of death

17. "chains" — **ἅλυσις** (*halusis*): plural, bonds, chains, or fetters; indicates hand and foot

18. "the door" — **τῆς θύρας** (*tes thuras*): depicts a large door locked with a bolt that slid through rings attached to the frame

19. "behold" — **ἰδού** (*idou*): bewilderment, shock, amazement, and wonder

20. "came upon" — **ἐφίστημι** (*ephistemi*): describes a surprise arrival accompanied with splendor and glory; a military word meaning to stand guard or to stay at one's post

21. "shined" — **λάμπω** (*lampo*): a beam of light

22. "prison" — **οἴκημα** (*oikema*): a prison cell, NOT the entire prison

23. "smote" — **πατάσσω** (*patasso*): to strike hard; to smite; to afflict

24. "saying" — **λέγων** (*legon*): repeatedly saying, over and over

25. "fell off" — **ἐξέπεσαν** (*exepesan*): to abruptly fall off; to fall off and hit the ground

26. "follow" — **ἀκολουθέω** (*akoloutheo*): to follow closely and obediently; to accompany; stick closely

27. "wist not" — **οὐκ ᾔδει** (*ouk edei*): emphatically did not comprehend; the full phrase says, "he followed and did not (**οὐκ**, ouk) know"

28. "ward" — **φυλακὴν** (*phulaken*): plural, guards

29. "the iron gate" — **τὴν πύλην τὴν σιδηρᾶν** (*ten pulen ten sideran*): literally, the gate -- the iron one

30. "which opened to them of his own accord" — **ἥτις αὐτομάτη ἠνοίγη αὐτοῖς** (*hetis automate enoige autois*) which automatically swung open by itself

31. "now" — **νῦν** (*nun*): right now, at this precise moment; a now moment

32. "the house" — **τὴν οἰκίαν** (*ten oikian*): definite article, THE house

33. "of Mary" — **τῆς Μαρίας** (*tēs Marias*): John Mark's mother, Barnabas' sister

34. "many" — **ἱκανός** (*hikanos*): plural, a considerable number; a substantial number; large numbers

35. "praying" — **προσευχή** (*proseuche*): pictures close, up-front, intimate contact; portrays an individual who desires to see his prayer answered so desperately that he is willing to surrender everything he owns in exchange for answered prayer; the concept of surrender

36. "knocked" — **κρούω** (*krouo*): to knock; to bang loudly

37. "continued knocking" — **ἐπέμενεν κρούων** (*epemenen krouon*): kept on banging and banging

38. "astonished" — **ἐξίστημι** (*existemi*): flabbergasted

39. "examined" — **ἀνακρίνω** (*anakrino*): to interrogate over and over

40. "abode" — **διατρίβω** (*diatribo*): to stay; to stay in a difficult place; to be stuck between two; implies this was not Peter's first choice, but what he had to do

SYNOPSIS

Many amazing events took place in the Upper Room in Jerusalem, including the Last Supper, the first Communion, Christ's high priestly prayer, and the outpouring of the Holy Spirit on the Day of Pentecost. Another important event is recorded in Acts 12. It states that after the apostle Peter had been arrested and imprisoned by King Herod, the believers joined together in prayer and began to intensely intercede for Peter's release.

God heard their cries and sent His angel to deliver Peter from the enemy's grasp. Instinctively, Peter knew where to go once he was released. He returned to the Upper Room in Mary's home to rejoin the believers who were gathered together in prayer. This was yet another Upper-Room reality for the record books.

The emphasis of this lesson:

When Peter was thrown into prison, the Church rallied together and intensely prayed for his release. Without ceasing, they sought God face-to-face, and He heard and answered their cries. The angel of the Lord supernaturally delivered Peter, and he rejoined fellow believers in the Upper Room.

Our final lesson is found in Acts 12 and details the story of Peter's arrest by King Herod and his miraculous deliverance by the angel of the Lord. In order to take in the rich truths of this story, let's begin in verse 1 and work our way through verse 19, identifying the meaning of the key words and phrases along the way.

> **"Now about that time Herod the king stretched forth his hands to vex certain of the church" (Acts 12:1).**

The words "stretched forth" here is the Greek word *epiballo*, which means *to lay his hand upon; to forcibly lay upon*. The phrase "his hands" is *tas cheiras* in Greek, and it indicates *meddling*. King Herod literally laid his meddling hands on certain people in the Church to "vex" them. The word "vex" is the Greek word *kakao*, and it means *to abuse; to harm; to injure; to maltreat or mistreat*.

This takes us to the word "church" — the Greek word *ekklesia*. It is from the word *ek*, which means *out*, and the word *kaleo*, which means *to call*. When the words are compounded, the new word *ekklesia* describes *a called, separated, and prestigious assembly*. In history, it denoted *a prestigious assembly who determined laws, debated public policy, formulated new policies, and ruled in judicial matters*. To be invited to this assembly was a great honor. In relation to the Church, the word *ekklesia* describes *the body of believers who have assembled to be God's representatives in every town, city, state, or nation; a body called to make decisions that affect the atmosphere of a region*. The devil hates the Church because it has power to stop his kingdom from advancing. Hence, he worked through Herod to vex the Church.

> **"And because he saw it pleased the Jews, he proceeded further to take Peter also. (Then were the days of unleavened bread)" (Acts 12:3).**

The phrase "proceeded further" is a translation of the Greek word *prosetheto*, which means *to proceed with a plan*. The word "take" is the Greek word *sullambano*, and it means *to conceive something; it is the same word used to describe a woman who has conceived a child in pregnancy.* Thus, Herod had *a well-conceived plan* to apprehend Peter. It was *a well-thought-out scheme that was growing and developing,* and it included seizing and doing away with Peter "also" — which means *even* Peter.

> **"And when he had apprehended him, he put him in prison, and delivered him to four quaternions of soldiers to keep him; intending after Easter to bring him forth to the people" (Acts 12:4).**

The Bible says Herod "apprehended" Peter, which is the Greek word *piadzo*, meaning *to catch; to lay hold of;* or *to seize.* Once Herod had physically seized Peter, he placed him in the custody of "four quaternions," which in Greek indicates two soldiers were confined to him (the prisoner) inside the prison cell and two others kept guard outside the prison doors.

King Herod was "intending after Easter" to deal with Peter. The word "intending" in Greek is *boulomai*, and it means he was *planning and counseling with himself to do something.* The word "Easter" here is a very poor translation. It is the Greek word *pascha*, which means *Passover*, not Easter. Verse 5 goes on to say:

> **"Peter therefore was kept in prison: but prayer was made without ceasing of the church unto God for him" (Acts 12:5).**

The word "kept" in Greek is *tereo*, and it pictures *soldiers who were faithful to their charge of keeping watch* regardless of assaults or the number of attackers they might encounter. As Peter was kept in prison, believers were in "prayer" for his release.

The word "prayer" is the Greek word *proseuche*, which is the word most widely used for prayer all through the New Testament. It pictures *close, up-front, intimate contact; coming close to express a wish, desire, prayer, or vow.* Often it is used to depict *a person who vowed to give something of great value to God in exchange for a favorable answer to prayer.* It portrays *an individual who desires to see his prayer answered so desperately that he is willing to surrender everything he owns in exchange for answered prayer.* Thus, the word *proseuche* — translated here as "prayer" — contained the concept of *surrender.*

The Church was praying "without ceasing," which means *fervently; in an extended, stretched-out manner; without let-up*. Believers were pressing in and pouring out their hearts "unto God." In Greek, the phrase "unto God" is *pros ton Theon*, and it means *face-to-face with God*. It is the same word used in John 1:1 where it says that the Word — Jesus — was "with God." Christians were earnestly seeking God face-to-face.

> **"And when Herod would have brought him forth, the same night Peter was sleeping between two soldiers, bound with two chains: and the keepers before the door kept the prison" (Acts 12:6).**

When it says, "Peter was sleeping," the word "sleeping" in Greek is *koimao-mai*, and it pictures *a deep sleep*. In fact, it sometimes refers to *the sleep of death*. The implication here is that Peter was not anxious or worried; he was sleeping soundly between two soldiers and was bound with "chains." The word "chains" — the Greek word *halusis* — is plural and describes *bonds, chains, or fetters*. The text says two chains, which indicates that Peter was bound hand and foot.

The Bible says, "...and the keepers before the door kept the prison" (Acts 12:6). Remember, there were four soldiers guarding Peter — two with him inside the prison and two just outside "the door." In Greek, "the door" is *tes thuras*, and it depicts *a large door locked with a bolt that slid through rings attached to the frame*. In the natural, Peter was held in a maximum security jail, and the likelihood of him getting out seemed impossible.

> **"And, behold, the angel of the Lord came upon him, and a light shined in the prison: and he smote Peter on the side, and raised him up, saying, Arise up quickly. And his chains fell off from his hands" (Acts 12:7).**

Notice the word "behold" here. It is the Greek word *idou*, and it describes *bewilderment, shock, amazement, and wonder*. As Luke was recounting this story, he used this word to convey that he was still quite stunned and amazed by what happened.

He said the angel of the Lord "came upon" Peter. In Greek, "came upon" is the word *ephistemi*, which describes *a surprise arrival accompanied with splendor and glory*. It is a military word meaning *to stand guard or to stay at one's post*. When the angel appeared, it totally took Peter off guard.

The Bible goes on to say, "a light shined in the prison." The word "shined" is the Greek word *lampo*, which describes *a beam of light*, and the word "prison" in Greek is *oikema*, which denotes *a prison cell*, NOT the entire prison.

Immediately, the angel "smote Peter on the side." The word "smote" is the Greek word *patasso*, and it means *to strike hard; to smite; to afflict*. Because Peter was sleeping so deeply, the angel had to hit him hard to wake him up. He then "...raised him up, saying, Arise up quickly...." The word "saying" here is the Greek word *legon*, which means the angel was *repeatedly saying, over and over,* "Arise, arise, arise!"

It then says, "...And his chains fell off from his hands." "Fell off" in Greek is the word *exepesan*, which means *to abruptly fall off; to fall off and hit the ground*. This was a supernatural event taking place.

> "And the angel said unto him, Gird thyself, and bind on thy sandals. And so he did. And he saith unto him, Cast thy garment about thee, and follow me. And he went out, and followed him; and wist not that it was true which was done by the angel; but thought he saw a vision" (Acts 12:8,9).

The angel of the Lord told Peter to "follow" him. "Follow" in Greek is the word *akoloutheo*, which means *to follow closely and obediently; to accompany; or to stick closely*. Peter's obedient actions demonstrate that sometimes we have to stay close to the Lord and do what He says even when we don't understand what is happening.

The Bible says Peter "...wist not that it was true which was done by the angel; but thought he saw a vision." The words "wist not" is a translation of the Greek words *ouk edei*, and it indicates that Peter *emphatically did not comprehend* what was going on. Nevertheless, he followed God's leading by following God's messenger.

> "When they were past the first and the second ward, they came unto the iron gate that leadeth unto the city; which opened to them of his own accord: and they went out, and passed on through one street; and forthwith the angel departed from him" (Acts 12:10).

The word "ward" here is the Greek word *phulaken*, which is the plural word for *guards*. Once Peter made it past the two soldiers that were guarding him inside the prison, he found himself before "the iron gate," which literally means *the gate — the iron one.* The fact that this gate was made of iron indicates it was very difficult to open. Nonetheless, it "opened to them of his own accord," which means *it automatically swung open by itself.*

Scripture goes on to say, "And when Peter was come to himself, he said, Now I know of a surety, that the Lord hath sent his angel, and hath delivered me out of the hand of Herod, and from all the expectation of the people of the Jews" (Acts 12:11). The word "now" is the Greek word *nun*, and it means *right now, at this precise moment.* Peter was experiencing a "now moment" — a moment when he came to his senses and realized the goodness of God was at work in his life.

"And when he had considered the thing, he came to the house of Mary the mother of John, whose surname was Mark; where many were gathered together praying" (Acts 12:12).

Interestingly, the phrase "the house" in Greek is *ten oikian*, and because it includes a definite article, it means *THE house.* Specifically, it was THE house "of Mary," which was John Mark's mother and Barnabas' sister. The Upper Room was located on the second or third floor of her home, and "...many were gathered together praying." The word "many" in Greek describes *a considerable number; a substantial number; or large numbers.*

Notice there were a substantial number of believers gathered together "praying." The word for "praying" here is the same word we saw earlier in verse 5 — the Greek word *proseuche.* It pictures *close, up-front, intimate contact.* It portrays believers desiring to see their prayers answered so desperately that they are willing to surrender everything they own in exchange for answered prayer.

Acts 12:13 says, "As Peter knocked at the door of the gate, a damsel came to hearken, named Rhoda." The word "knocked" here is the Greek word *krouo*, which means *to knock or to bang loudly.* The Bible goes on to say, "And when she knew Peter's voice, she opened not the gate for gladness, but ran in, and told how Peter stood before the gate. And they said unto her, Thou art mad. But she constantly affirmed that it was even so. Then said they, It is his angel" (Acts 12:14,15).

Miraculously, God had answered their prayers, but they had a very hard time believing it.

"But Peter continued knocking: and when they had opened the door, and saw him, they were astonished" (Acts 12:16).

Notice the words "continued knocking" — the Greek words *epemenen krouon*. It means Peter *kept on banging and banging*. When the believers inside finally opened the door and saw him themselves, they were "astonished," which means they were simply *flabbergasted*.

Verse 17 says, "But he [Peter], beckoning unto them with the hand to hold their peace, declared unto them how the Lord had brought him out of the prison. And he said, Go shew these things unto James, and to the brethren. And he departed, and went into another place."

At that time, James was the leader of the church in Jerusalem. The fact that Peter instructed the believers to share with James what had happened shows his willing submission and accountability to Church leadership. Even Peter — one of the original twelve trained by Jesus — respected spiritual authority. In the same way, we must submit to the spiritual authority God has placed over us.

After Peter shared what had happened with the believers in the Upper Room, "…he departed, and went to another place" (Acts 12:17).

"And when Herod had sought for him, and found him not, he examined the keepers, and commanded that they should be put to death. And he went down from Judaea to Caesarea, and there abode" (Acts 12:19).

The word "examined" in this verse is the Greek word *anakrino*, which means *to interrogate over and over*. After King Herod intensely interrogated the soldiers who had been assigned to guard Peter, he had them executed for their failure to keep him in custody. Meanwhile, Peter went down to the coastal city of Caesarea and there he "abode," which means *to stay*; *to stay in a difficult place*; or *to be stuck between two places*. The use of this term implies this was not Peter's first choice, but it was what he had to do for that moment.

Friend, all these remarkable events we have been studying — including prayer for Peter's release from the clutches of Herod — all took place in the Upper Room of Mary's home. When she invited Jesus to come in and use her home whenever He needed it, He accepted her invitation, and His Spirit never left. What will Jesus do when you open *your home* to Him?

Only God knows for sure. But one thing is certain — He will fill your space with His Holy Spirit and your life will be forever changed!

STUDY QUESTIONS

Study to shew thyself approved unto God, a workman that needeth
not to be ashamed, rightly dividing the word of truth.
— 2 Timothy 2:15

1. As you come to the end of this study on *Upper Room Realities*, what is one of your greatest takeaways?

2. Peter was held in a maximum-security prison — the chance of him getting out seemed impossible. Are you in a situation like Peter's? Do you feel trapped? What does God say about situations like this in Luke 1:37; Matthew 19:26; and Genesis 18:14? How do these verses, along with God's promise in Ephesians 3:20, give you new hope for Him to act?

3. The Bible says that God sent an angel to deliver Peter from prison. What do you know about angels? What other stories from Scripture come to mind in which angels helped people? According to Hebrews 1:14 and Psalm 91:11 and 12, what are a couple of ways angels help us?

PRACTICAL APPLICATION

But be ye doers of the word, and not hearers only,
deceiving your own selves.
— James 1:22

1. From the moment Peter was awakened by the angel to the time he was unchained and led out through the prison gates, he was in a daze and thought he was dreaming. Yet, although he didn't fully understand what was happening, he obediently followed God's messenger. Are you experiencing something that you don't fully understand yet you know God is in it? Take a few moments to explain what is happening and how God seems to be leading you through the situation. Are you following Him and cooperating with His Holy Spirit? Is there anything He has asked you to do that you are being reminded of right now?

2. After Peter had been miraculously delivered from maximum security, he finally came to his senses and realized what had happened. Have you ever experienced a "now moment" like this — when you really woke up to the reality of what God had done in your life? Or maybe you were like the believers in the Upper Room who prayed and couldn't believe their prayers were answered. Take a moment to recall how God miraculously intervened.

3. Just as the Holy Spirit moved in the Upper Room on the Day of Pentecost, He desires to move in your home. In the same way He filled the 120, He desires to fill you and every member of your family! Are you ready to surrender your home and your family to the Lord?